Arms of the Burgh of Old Aberdeen.

THE STORY OF
OLD ABERDEEN

BY

KATHERINE E. TRAIL

ABERDEEN : D. WYLLIE & SON.

1929

Dedication

To Brenda,

WITHOUT WHOSE HELP THIS BOOK
WOULD NOT HAVE BEEN PRINTED.

ALL PROFITS WILL BE GIVEN
TO THE CATHEDRAL RESTORATION FUND.

FOREWORD.

This little book has been published in the hope that it will tell the story of an Ancient Burgh, which, owing to the relentless march of circumstances, has been incorporated in the neighbouring large town. The author hopes that it may interest the youth of Old Aberdeen, recall to many now far scattered the home of their childhood, and revive in the minds of those who are going down the hill the days of long ago when we had our own Provost and Town Council and were very proud of our independence.

It is a very simple statement, and does not attempt to answer any knotty points. If it succeeds in its purpose of interesting the younger generation, it will amply accomplish the wish of its author, who was born in Old Aberdeen, and has lived her whole life in the little place she loves so well.

She desires to acknowledge the very great help she has received from the late Mr. P. J. Anderson, from Miss Best and Dr. W. Douglas Simpson.

June, 1929.

CONTENTS.

LIST OF ILLUSTRATIONS.

OLD ABERDEEN

CHAPTER I.

FROM a very early date the burgh of Old Aberdeen, or Auld Aberdon, has stood upon the wooded height overlooking the Don, facing the waters of the North Sea on the East and protected on the West by the great woods of Forrester and Stocket Hills. The situation was well chosen; the river abounded in salmon and the woods were full of game. Both sea and forest afforded protection to the early settlers, to whom legend attributes the date of 3489 years after the Creation of the World! However that may be, tradition is busy again in the 6th Century, when we are told that St. Machar, sent out by St. Columba from Iona to found a church on the bank of a river which by its windings formed a shepherd's crook, decided that here he had found the place of which he was in search. He chose the high bank above the river where the Cathedral now stands; here St. Machar built the first little church, here he and his disciples settled, and here the Message of the Cross has been preached ever since. We know that St. Machar died in France in 594 after a visit to Rome, in the time of Gregory the Great. We have no idea who succeeded him, but we have every reason to believe that the missionary work was carried on.

Indeed, the fact that in 1136 David I., the " Sair Saint for Scotland," resolved to transfer to the church at Old Aberdon the Bishop's See from Mortlach, in Banffshire, would seem to prove that the Church and Mission had grown in importance. At the time of the transfer the settlement consisted of a " village of four ploughs," known as the Kirkton of Seaton. The charter of King David endowed the Bishopric with the whole village, a very large tract of country and the tithes of land, and money belonging to the King. The first Bishop of the newly created Cathedral was Nectanus, but what his church was like we have no idea. It became, however, the centre of religious life in the North-East of Scotland, and its power over the little community of Old Aberdeen was supreme, as its Bishops were at the head of its secular as well as its spiritual interests. Indeed, the Cathedral played so large a part in the affairs of Old Aberdeen that it requires a whole chapter to itself; but it may be interesting here to consider the buildings that housed the Bishop and his clergy in the immediate vicinity of the church.

Of these buildings there is hardly any trace now, but from the accounts given by Orem and Spalding we can form a fairly accurate idea of what they must have been.

We know that the Cathedral precincts were surrounded by a wall in which were four gates, the chief of which on the South opened into the Chanonry or direct access to the Cathedral. This gate was called Cluny's Gate, and was still standing in the beginning of the 18th century. Originally Cluny's Gate was surmounted by the effigy of the Virgin and the Arms of Old Aberdeen, while an inscription upon it ran :—

" Hac ne vade via, nisi dixeris Ave Maria.
Invenies veniam sic salutando Mariam."

[" Pass not this way unless you say, ' Hail, Mary.'
By such a salutation you will obtain pardon."]

At the Reformation, the effigy of the Virgin was destroyed, but the Arms of the city were still distinctly to be seen, and the gate was entire in 1725. Probably the gate took its name from the Laird of Cluny, whose house and garden, the most beautiful in the town, were just inside it. The name was preserved in the narrow road known as Cluny's Wynd, leading to Woodside, which has been swept away by the city improvements.

Another gate giving direct access to the North was on Tillydrone Hill, fairly near the top and close to the conical mound which tradition claims to have been heaped up by the nuns, who as penance for some sin were compelled to carry up the soil from the low ground of Seaton in their aprons.

The third gate was close to the little village of Seaton and opened into the Bishop's garden.

The fourth gate was at the end of the chaplainry, close to the chaplain's chambers. It was built by William Stewart, Bishop of Aberdeen, Chancellor of Scotland.

Like Cluny's Gate, it was standing in the 18th century. Within these gates were the Bishop's palace, the manses of the Prebends, the convent of the Holy Sisters of St. Katherine, and Bishop Dunbar's Hospital for Men.

Of all these buildings not a trace is left, but a short account of what we know of them from history and legend may prove of general interest.

The Bishop's palace stood a little to the north-east of the Cathedral. We are told that the palace was in the shape of a large court, having four towers, one at each corner. It contained one large hall and several rooms. An underground passage led from it to the Chancellor's house, of which only the outer wall still stands. The garden lay to the East, between the palace and the chaplain's chambers, of which the southern-most still stands in good condition, the steep roof with its crow's steps, and Bishop Dunbar's mitre, cut in the stone on the wall, giving us a clue to the date. The palace possessed also a summer house three stories high, from which a magnificent view of the sea could be obtained. In the centre of the courtyard was a deep well, and on the north side of the garden was a dovecot. The palace, judging by the inventory of the furniture and appointments, left by Bishop Gordon, 1577, the last Catholic Bishop, does not seem to have been quite worthy of its name. We are told that the wardrobe contained " five pairs of sheets one thereof sewed with silk, eight pillows great and small, two pairs of fustian blankets, one pair double woollen blankets and nine feather beds with bolsters; a great arras bed, with roof and head, with the King's Arms and Bishop Elphinstone's fringed; two arras

St. Machar's Cathedral, with Elphinstone's Tower.

beds with the same Bishop's Arms, a white Ireland plaid corset with black rings; an old counter cloth of Buchan weaving; a great press of oak and fir, a great long chest of oak; the pipes of an aqua vitae vat.

" In the chamber; one standing bed of oak, one long saddle seat of oak, one small counter, a portail.

" In the chapel chamber; one large oak bed with roof of arras and head fringe, an oak screen, an iron chandelier.

" In the great chamber; a large standing bed of oak, two counters, a long saddle seat, two forms of oak, a great portail, a brass chandelier suspended; eight small chandeliers, two iron fire racks, four cushions of needlework; the chamber hangings of sey, pale red, blue and yellow.

" In the closet; a standing bed of oak with curtains of sey, red, green and blue; a chair of ease, a small chair; a counter with cloth cover, a large saddle bed of oak, a cup almory of oak.

" In the study; a fire screen; an old saddle seat; a press of oak for breeches; a small oak chest for letters; a table for the crucifix; three boards with trestles and forms; a counter; a harthorn horse, a quhitstone chained with iron; an oak chair."

I have quoted the inventory in full, as it is interesting to compare it with what would be considered necessary for the furnishing of a Bishop's palace in our day.

Evidently this was the second palace on this site. The first was built in 1329 by Bishop Alexander Kininmonth, but was destroyed in 1336 by the English, who, according to Kennedy, " set fire to the burgh of Aberdeen." For more than one hundred years the Bishops occupied the palace on the island in the Bishop's Loch. In 1459 Bishop Thomas Spens rebuilt the palace in the Cathedral grounds, which was then the permanent residence of the Bishops till it, too, was demolished by the English in 1651, many of the stones being carried off to complete the fortifications on Castle Hill.

The Girth Cross, or Sanctuary Cross, stood on the Dovecot Green. William the Lion had ordered that every cathedral in Scotland should have such a sanctuary erected in its precincts. After the Reformation the Girth Cross was removed from the Cathedral and placed at the top of the High Street, where the Town House now stands. It was used as a Market Cross, and many allusions are made to it in the history of Old Aberdeen. At the top of the Cross was the figure of the Virgin Mary, destroyed in the days of the Reformation ; below were the Royal Arms and those of Bishop Dunbar, Bishop Stewart and Bishop Gordon. Spalding tells us of a pretty Candlemas custom, when the bairns of the Old Town Grammar School carrying lighted candles marched round the Cross in a long procession " blithe eneuch." The leader, or Candlemas King, then climbed the Cross and fixed his blazing torch on the top. At the time when Spalding wrote the chosen leader was John Keith, brother of the Lord Marischal, and Spalding can only prophesy evil for the " dour Covenanter "; but we may be pardoned for

Bishop Dunbar's Hospital.

thinking of the joy that such an occasion brought to the children, whose lives must inevitably have been darkened by the times in which they lived. Not long ago the base of the Cross with the Arms of the Bishops was found in a neighbouring smithy, the hole for the Cross filled with scrap iron and rubbish. It is now preserved in the museum of King's College.

Very early mention is made of a Song School, which seems to have stood in close proximity to the Cathedral, but of which we have no exact information till 1642, when Dr. Guild, Principal of King's College, built a new school upon the site of the Bishop's Dovecot.

Another very interesting building stood near the Cathedral—the hospital founded by Bishop Gavin Dunbar, in 1531, for twelve poor men. It is described as " having twelve little chambers with as many little chimneys for a little fire in each of them." It had also a common hall and an oratory. It was intended by Bishop Dunbar to be a home for such men " as were of a good conversation," who had lived on the Bishop's lands or who had done work about the kirk, the Bishop's palace, Prebends' manses, or the Bridge of Dee. Failing these, old soldiers or blind or lame men might look to the hospital as an asylum. All the inmates had to be over sixty years of age; each man received twelve merks four times a year and a white coat annually. A very strict time-table was laid down. At 8 a.m. they must go to the oratory for their devotions, at 11 a.m. to mass in the Cathedral, at 3 p.m. devotions in the oratory, at 5 p.m. and again at 8 p.m. to devotions in the oratory.   Dinner was served in the hall at one o'clock; each man had supper in his own room at eight o'clock.   Exercises in the garden formed the day's diversion.   No woman was ever to be seen in the hospital.   The hospital stood to the west of the Cathedral in the grounds of Tillydrone until 1786, when it was handed over to James of Seaton in exchange for a house in Don Street, still called the Bede House. We have no evidence that this was ever inhabited by the Bedesmen. The endowment remains; eighteen old men receive 12/- monthly and a salmon a year from the fund known as the Bede, or Bead, Fund.

Close to the Cathedral in the Chanonry, or Chanry, were built the lodgings or manses of the Prebends.   Each of these had its garden, " little taills," as Orem calls them.   There were about twenty of these manses; the Prebends formed the Bishop's Chapter.   They were parsons of country churches, but they had to live near the Cathedral that they might be ready to attend when required by the Bishop.   That the manses in which they lived were not very large is shown not only by their total destruction but also by an inventory of the furniture each Prebend was expected to leave for his successor, viz. :—

" In the dining-hall : a large table, a silver spoon, a tablecloth and a towel. In the bedroom : a couch, a pair of linen sheets and two pairs of blankets. In the kitchen : an iron pot, an iron chain or kettle crook and a dish clout " !

We can very easily understand how much power was in the hands of the Bishop and his Chapter, living thus apart from and yet in the centre of the community, over which they ruled as Superiors, choosing the Provost, Baillies and Council.

CHAPTER II.

In a Charter dated 1498, James I. created the " Ville of Aberdon " into a " Free Burgh of Barony " with full power to its inhabitants to buy and sell wines, wax, cloth, woollen and linen, and to have and keep bakers, brewers, and butchers " as well of fleshes as of fisches " and other craftsmen. He decreed that every Monday should be Market Day and that two Fairs should be held annually—one on Skeir Thursday, that is the day before Good Friday, and another on St. Luke's Day, which was to last for eight days. The Skeir Thursday Fair must have faded away long ago, but St. Luke's Fair, or the Aulton Market, was, until quite recent years, the most ardently looked-forward-to day of the year by all the Old Aberdeen children. Two or three days before the market caravans began to arrive and take up their stances. Wonderful prodigies of Nature, such as the fat woman, the two-headed boy, and the boneless man, were exhibited; merry-go-rounds with their blaring music, cocoanut shies and rifle ranges were largely patronised by young and old; and the fun of the fair was fast and furious. The Aulton Market, too, is a thing of the past, but I am sure that old inhabitants have many a kindly recollection of it and the merry moments they spent there.

The Trades of Old Aberdeen consisted of hammermen (including smiths), wrights and coopers, tailors, shoemakers, weavers, and fleshers. They seem to have been quite flourishing; in the Town House are preserved some wooden chairs with the insignia of the Trades cut on their backs. The Trades were a source of revenue to the Cathedral, as they contributed half the entry money paid to them by the craftsmen. They helped also with the salary of the master of the Song School, and subscribed to the building of the new school. No craftsman could become a member of a trade without having first satisfied the deacon of his ability, and no person not a member of the Trade could make or sell goods in the city. So much for liberty in those days! The deacon convener was chosen by each of the Trades in turn. Early in their history we find them coming into collision with their brethren the Trades in Aberdeen. They decided to have nothing to do with the latter without special consent of the whole body; but this decision by no means ended the quarrel, which raged for many years. In their difficulties the Old Aberdeen Trades were greatly helped by Mr. John Paton of Grandhome and Mr. George Gordon of Rainnieshill. The gratitude of the Trades took what to us seems rather a curious, not to say depressing, form! One of the privileges of the Trades was to hire out mort cloths for funerals. Of these they possessed several of various qualities, the price varying with the quality. One was kept and lent gratis to any poor people who could not afford to pay. A minute of 1720 records that for the good services done by the afore-mentioned gentlemen, " the Convener and haill members of Court bind and oblidge them and their successors in Office that the sds. John

Paton and Mr. George Gordon, their wifes and children, when dead and unmarried, shall have the benefit and priviledge of the best mort cloathes belonging to the sds. Trades and that gratis, without paying any dues, therefore and this to be extended to the heir or heires of the sds. families in all tyme coming allenarly, gratis as said is." Aberdeen Trades continued to be most annoying, however. Old Aberdeen Trades petitioned Government to overthrow a decree of the Sheriff, as the members greatly feared that should the oppression from New Aberdeen be allowed to continue they " may at last bring us to be in no better caice than as if we were ther suburbs, as they are pleased to term us in ther vexatious process." Apparently Aberdeen ceased from troubling, and the Old Aberdeen Trades were allowed to carry on their callings peacefully. All the Trades had seats or " lofts " in the Cathedral; they were expected to attend service regularly and to accompany the convener to every funeral. A tax was levied for the " pretended Prince of Wales " in 1745, and this at a time when they were so hard pressed for money that they were obliged to resolve to give no more entertainments out of the funds. Recognising the very good work done by the Infirmary, however, a donation was unanimously voted for its funds. The Trades showed their generosity, too, by sending help to a poor weaver in Aberdeen who had been " burnt out." Surely this was heaping coals of fire on Aberdeen !

The Trades determined to do something for their women, and on some property they possessed in the

Chanonry they built a hospital to house ten women— either widows or spinsters in necessitous circumstances belonging to members of any of the Trades Guilds. The hospital was built in 1711, but apparently was not very popular, as we read in 1765 that the widows preferred to take the very small endowment and find their own homes. This did not appeal to the members of the Trades, as it does to us, and they decreed that the endowment would not be given to anyone not resident in the hospital, " it being to the loss of the house greatly to want possessors, who must burn fire therein." In 1792 the house was sold for £50 sterling. It is interesting to note that all the accounts are made out in sterling money from now on.

This Trades Hospital was the forerunner of Mitchell's Hospital in the Chanonry, better known as the Old Maids' Hospital. Founded in 1801 by David Mitchell, a native of Old Aberdeen, it was intended for five widows and five unmarried daughters of trade and merchant burgesses of Old Aberdeen. His intention was that the inmates should live a more or less communal life, be dressed alike in deep blue, and he would prefer that if possible they should all be of the families of Forbes or Mitchell. With a profound knowledge of human nature, Mr. Mitchell says, " As it is impossible to keep order and regularity among ten women except one of them have a superiority over the rest, I appoint the trustees to choose a sensible, discreet woman to be the Governess or Mistress of the Hospital, to whom all must promise due obedience." All who could earn a little either by spinning or knitting were expected to give half their earnings to the hospital, the other half they might keep for snuff or tobacco—surely a modern touch this! Strict rules as to diet were laid down. Boiled beef and greens were to be enjoyed for dinner three times a week, when the price of beef was not more than 4d. a pound; when it exceeded that, beef must be restricted to twice a week. Dinner on the remaining days was to consist of fish or eggs. One bottle of beer was allowed each inmate for dinner and supper except on salt fish days, when two extra bottles were to be divided among them all. Breakfast and supper consisted of porridge or sowens. The cooking was to be done by the inmates in turn, and Mr. Mitchell concludes his deed of bene-faction by a pious hope that " the women would always behave in a Christian, decent and sisterly manner to each other and would be thankful to God for the quiet and comfort they enjoyed without being under the disagreeable necessity of supplicating these blessings from strangers or cruel-hearted relations." Something of a philosopher as well as a benefactor, this Mr. Mitchell. The hospital has still the same appear-ance as when it was built, but the internal arrange-ments have had to be entirely altered to suit the altered conditions of to-day. Four delightful homes, self-contained, fitted with bathrooms and electric light, are provided rent free to the widows and unmarried daughters of burgesses of Old Aberdeen. The spirit, if not the text, of Mr. Mitchell's benefaction is most carefully preserved, and the privilege of possessing such a home in these days of housing shortage is greatly appreciated by the lucky few. It would be well if others would imitate Mr. Mitchell's example.

There has always been a theory that the dwellers in the Chanonry were not quite the same as other people, a theory that was well illustrated when a stranger, asking the way to the Old Maids' Hospital, was told, " Oh, that's the hoosie in atween the twa daft Chairlies.'' The allusion was to Mr. Charles Burnett, who occupied 8 Chanonry, now belonging to the Botanic Garden, and to Mr. Charles Leslie, who lived in 11 Chanonry.

Mr. Charles Burnett, brother of the famous Laird of Kemnay, spent the latter years of his life in Old Aberdeen. Extraordinarily kind-hearted, he was a very good hater, and he had no regard for what anyone might say of him. He had a passion for flowers, and had he had a scientific training he might have done some very good work. He succeeded in producing a number of fine hybrids, but, unfortunately, was never able to account for them. His appearance was most picturesque, and he was a familiar figure in the Old Town, with his long silvery hair and beard and flowing Highland cloak. His brother, Erskine, lived at one time in Don Street. He shared the same love of Nature, and used to tell a tale of how, wandering in the woods one Sunday, he saw a kestrel's nest at the top of a tree. He did not think it right to take the eggs on a Sunday, so he quietly settled himself at the foot to wait for Monday morning. Immediately after midnight he climbed the tree and secured two eggs, which he placed in his mouth. Chilled by the long wait, he slipped coming down, fell heavily, broke his leg, and—what to him was far worse—the eggs also.

Opposite Mr. Burnett lived the Misses Gerard, daughters of Professor Gilbert Gerard, whose connection with Aberdeen and the Universities was a very close one. Their grandfather, Alexander Gerard, was Professor of Divinity in King's College, after having been one of the Regents in Marischal College. In his manse, the Chaplainry, he entertained Dr. Johnson and Boswell. In the Senatus Room of King's College are portraits of Professor Alexander Gerard, his wife, and Professor Gilbert Gerard. In the portraits of father and son we see a strong resemblance. Both faces are very gentle, sensitive and refined. Professor Alexander Gerard is also depicted in the famous caricature, the " Sapient Septem Viri." Gilbert Gerard was appointed Professor of Greek in 1790, and succeeded his father as Professor of Divinity in 1795. In 1803 he was appointed to the Second Charge of St. Machar's Cathedral. Pluralities were evidently permitted in those days, and doubtless he required all the income he could get for the upkeep of his large family of five sons and six daughters. The house, No. 6 Chanonry, was bought by his widow and inhabited by her and her daughters, none of whom married. The last two passed away only in the later years of the 19th Century. Old Aberdeen has often been compared to Cranford, and truly Misses Helen and Marjory Gerard might have stepped straight from the pages of that famous book. They had inherited literary tastes from father and grandfather, to whom also they owed very refined, sensitive, musical natures. The family love of being painted showed itself in them by their love of being photographed. They were always taken at a window, Helen holding the harp, which she played beautifully. The ladies lived a life absolutely apart from the life of the ordinary world. Their days were passed in semi-darkness, all the blinds were kept pulled down, and they never went outside in daylight. This peculiarity gave rise to much speculation, some people holding that they were Albinos. It was said that they had had a sort of sunstroke when crossing the Bridge of Don one April afternoon, after which they never again faced the sun's rays. Their dread of light was so great that they would sometimes go about the house under the shade of an umbrella or parasol. The close vicinity of the gymnasium rather troubled them, and forced them to take refuge in the back of their house. The atmosphere of their rooms was just like themselves, reminiscent of the days that are gone.

Absolutely different from the Misses Gerard were the Misses Forbes who lived at No. 10 Chanonry, up the long walk. They also were two delightful ladies of the old school, cultured and artistic, who spent their winters in Italy and brought home to the little Old Town a breath of a wider air.

Can anyone wonder that the influence of two such homes as those of the Misses Gerard and the Misses Forbes, combined with the culture and learning of the Professors, and the shrewd, kindly Scottish wit of the Misses Leslie, who lived at Powis House, must have permeated the whole of Old Aberdeen and have given some grounds for the feeling, so often expressed, that Old Aberdeen considered itself highly superior to New Aberdeen. Contact between the two towns was very slight. There were no means of communication, except by walking or hiring a cab. All the necessities of life could be bought or made in the Old Town; the large families of the ministers and professors, together with the boys of the gymnasium, formed a very happy community. Small wonder, then, that Old Aberdeen considered itself as a town apart, and less wonder that the inhabitants of New Aberdeen, looking at it with jealous eyes, made nasty remarks about the conceit and superiority of those who lived in " Sleepy Hollow." Well, well, these happy days are past, and no longer can the preacher pray, as Dr. Trail did in King's College Chapel, that a blessing might " rest upon this and the neighbouring city."

Of Dr. Jamieson in the manse, I suppose more stories have been told than of any other clergyman in the Church of Scotland. There was a spice of excitement about going to church when he was preaching, for one never knew what he would say, though one was quite certain it would not be what anyone else would have said! When Dr. Jamieson was in the manse, the Principal's house in the Chanonry was occupied by Principal Pirie. He, too, was not like other men, in that he had a bigger heart, a kindlier, quicker wit, than is given to most of the sons of men. His daughter is still with us, and it will be a black day for Old Aberdeen when Miss Pirie, beloved of all, high and low, for her great gifts of heart and mind, is taken away.

The Gymnasium, a most flourishing boarding school for boys, was also in the Chanonry. It was started by Dr. Anderson, better known as " Govie," whose extreme absence of mind was only rivalled by his kindness of heart. I think there is no doubt that the dwellers in the Chanonry, not so long ago, were not quite like other people, in that they were more original.

CHAPTER III.

BEHIND the Chanonry to the West was the Loch of Old Aberdeen. Probably the loch had been a peat moss, for we find that it was regularly let to various tenants. Water very likely collected in the hollows, for one of the tenants is to be allowed 6/8 for every animal that fell into the loch. Spalding gives us rather an interesting little touch when he says " that no maws or gulls were seen in the lochs of New or Old Aberdeen since the beginning of these troubles (1642-1645) and coming of soldiers to Aberdeen, who before flocked and clucked in so great abundance."

In 1662 James Gordon of Seaton drained the loch, and during the " space of his tack " he had plentiful crops of corn upon it. At the end of his lease the town took it into their own hands and rouped it annually.

We find many references to the loch in the Town Council minutes, which show us something of the life led by our ancestors. Washing day occasioned much trouble in Old Aberdeen then, as now! The water question was always a difficult one, and was a main argument for the union of New Aberdeen and Old Aberdeen in much later years. Springs in the fields to the west supplied a certain amount of water, and there were three public pumps — one in College Bounds, one at the foot of the Chaplainry Brae, and one in Chanonry just outside the churchyard! In addition, a small burn flowed from the loch, joined the Powis burn, crossed College Bounds, and so down University Road to the Links. It was evidently the custom to go out with washing tubs to the nearest point of the burn, there light one's fire, and proceed with the weekly wash. This custom much annoyed the Provost and Council, who in 1689 enact statute and ordaine " that no person nor persones within the Old Towne of Aberdeen or Chanonrie wasch any cloathes or anything els at any pairt of the Chanonrie from the head to the fute thereof, bot onlie at the backsyde, nixt the loch and that they sett ther fyres and wasching vessels ther, and throw out ther foull water on the South syde of the entrie of the said channel . . . as lykwyse that no persone wasch at any pairt of the Powies Burne . . . and siclyke dischairges all persones to Tramp and wash in tubs upon any pairt of the High street from the on [sic] end of the towne to the other and that under the penaltie of fourtie shilling Scot to be payit to the Thesr. for the use of the towne, and tuell shilling Scots to the officiars who are heirby impowered to poynd ther cloathes and wasching tubs thairfor whill they be payit and that for each transgressione toties quoties."

As we have seen, the Bishops of St. Machar's Cathedral were the Superiors of the City of Old Aberdeen, and as such nominated the Provost, Baillies, Sergeants, etc. The Council meetings were held in the Consistory House, which seems to have served as the Song School as well. The minutes give us a clear idea of a life very different from the life of to-day.

Apparently Old Aberdeen had been a walled city, as we find an Order in 1603, "Every indweller in this towne sall bigge upe the bak dykis for outhaulding of strangiers," and very severe punishment is threatened to anyone giving shelter to a stranger during the years of plague, 1604-1606.

The beer brewed in the Old Town was of a very fine quality, and many laws were passed by the Council as to the hours of selling. No drink is to be sold after 9 p.m., and none is to be sold at any time to the children attending the school. In 1605 a law was passed which might well be applied to the youth of to-day—" Na yeoung man within this towne that hes not ane hous or rent of his awn sall play at cartis, tabills, or dyss " upon penalty of forty shillings, or else sit upon the stool of repentance !

One of the town's officials was the " Scourger," an individual who may fairly be said to have earned his pay of 8/- a week. He is charged with the duty of keeping the town free of beggars — which must have been a very difficult job if we may judge from the number of edicts regarding them in the Town Council minutes. Probably the question of unemployment was, in a smaller way, quite as acute in the days of our forefathers as it is to-day ; but in the 17th century there was no dole—it was " work " or " clear out." Yet the Town Council was not hard-hearted, for they drew a distinction between the able-bodied poor and those who were unable to work. To the latter was granted permission not only to remain in the town but " they shall come preceiselie and get

almes at the yetis of honest men on such dayes allanerlie as they have or shall appoint for dealing thair
almes and shall not molest thair yetis nor housses
upon uther dayes under the pain of chastisment and
removall aff of the towne." These privileged poor
were known by the " townes marke on thair breastes,
to wit ane floure de luce in leid."

The poor of the parish had a privilege granted to
them also, which reads strangely in our ears, " They
sall have thair awin marke viz., ane star in leid and
sall have libertie to cum into the towne allanerlie on
Sunday to heir the preiching and with this provisioun
that thai come in to the kirke befoir the reading of
the text and byd thair the time of the sermon, and if
they be found on any weeke dayes in the towne in that
caice to be punished as stranger beggars and chased
away by the Scourger." Evidently the beggars were
apt to be contumelious at times and to refuse to be
chased away, in which case the Scourger " sall
requyre two of the nearest neighbours to that place
quhair the sturdy beggar is found to assist him, and
in caice they refuis ther helps . . . they are
ordainit to pay for thair penaltie thrie weekes wages
toties quoties."

Scourging through the town was a fairly common
punishment, but one which, so far as I can discover,
was reserved for women. In almost all instances cases
of theft are punished in this manner, and the victim
is scourged through the whole town between the
church and the Spital and then banished. Should she
ever reappear she will be " brunit without doome or

law." Some of the thefts seem to us hardly worthy of such a dire sentence; for instance, we have in 1671 the case of Christian Sutherland, a married woman, who pleads guilty to stealing " ane hank of fingering yarn from John Ross, Sacrist, King's College, as also ane long fisch and four cutts of salmon, all upon the fifth day of June." One wonders what had driven this poor woman to such an orgy of wickedness, all on a summer's day. Her punishment, which followed her sentence two days later, was " at two o'clock in the afternoon to be scourged through the town, banished, and never to be sene again ther upon pain of instant burning." The " good old days " left something to be desired.

We are told that " skolding and trubling of the towne be flyting is ane commond cours in Old Aberdeen," and it is decided that the guilty party shall pay a fine and " sall remain ane hour in the Gogis at the Cross." As the Scourger acted as Hangman too, we must allow that his job was no sinecure.

The domestic question raised its head even then. How true, O Solomon, there is nothing new under the sun. In 1643 we find the terms of an apprenticeship between William Dunn and Jean Mukart, his spous, on the one hand, and Elspet Gilcryst on the other. It is to last for seven years, and Elspet is to be provided " in mait, claith and intertenement," and is to be " learnt to waif schanks " in return for her work. Apparently clothing was part of the regular wages, for another entry tells us of Margaret Ellis receiving for her half-year's fee " four merks of silver withe cot

and sleives, ane pair of schone, and ane new sark."
Servants not quite content would seem to have had a
trick of leaving their places without due notice, as the
Town Council issues an order that every man or
woman servant shall, six weeks before Whitsunday and
Martinmas, "give lawful and timous advertisement to
thir maisters or maistresses" whether they intend to
stay for another six months. This is evidently the
origin of a custom, now practically dead, known as
Speaking Day, which was universal six weeks before
the term not so very long ago.

CHAPTER IV.

THE University has played such an important part in the history of the town that a whole chapter must be devoted to it. I should like, however, here to draw the attention of my readers to the fact that the University was founded by Bishop Elphinstone, the most famous of the Cathedral Bishops, and, indeed, the foremost man of his time in Scotland. Bishop Elphinstone constituted himself and his successors in office Chancellors of the University. The Cathedral thus was head, not only of religious and secular affairs but of educational also. We shall see as we go on how the Church gradually lost this supreme power after the Reformation, but in Old Aberdeen at least there was always a very real spirit of concord between the Church, the Town Council and the University.

The upbringing and education of the children were matters of great concern to the Town Council, for till the days of the School Board, the schools were under the direct supervision of the ministers and kirk sessions throughout the country. Doubtless the youth of that day got into mischief just as it does to-day. In 1606 the " haill Infantorie within this towne sick as Arthure alias Wee Auld Thomas Robertson . . . sall compeer befoir the pulpit and sit down on thair knies, ask first God the congregation and thair fatheirs forgievance and sycklik it is statuit and ordained that the fathers of the said Infanterie sall within ilk fyfteen dayis delait thair bairnes liffis and behaweor to the bailzes.''

We have no record of what the heinous sin of the poor, little Infanterie consisted to bring down upon them such dire punishment. To have to give an account to the baillies every fortnight of the doings of their children must have been a sore trial to the fathers.

It was evidently time to see about a new school-house, and the Council, which helped to pay the rent of the master, now resolved to give as much help as it could towards a new building. It was decided to build a new school of two storeys, the lower to be the ward-house or prison, the upper to be the Town Council room and school. The necessity for some sort of wardhouse is very apparent, as there was no prison for incarcerating persons guilty '' of whatsumever crimes, whether thieving, scolding, cursing, swearing, Sabbath-breaking or the lyke '' except '' the Church,'' and it was felt by the Session that the house appointed for public worship and the service of God should no longer be '' a receptacle for such persones.''

The fee for being taught to read was fixed by the Provost and Baillies at 3/4. The Song School was regularly visited by them; the appointment of the master, who was also clerk, was made by the Session. In spite of the very small salary paid to the master, education must have been considered a paying profession, as several private schools were started, to the damage of the public school. The Provost and Baillies, taking this into their consideration, forbade parents to send their children to any but the public Musick School.

Some of the masters sought to eke out their income by various means, one even keeping the Public Change House. This did not commend itself to the Fathers of the town, who decreed that in future no master of the school shall keep " een common Change." Baillie William Baxter dissented.

The Grammar School, however, must have been quite a flourishing institution by the end of the 17th century. It can be seen in Slezer's Picture, a small building in front of King's College. In 1675 its fees were fixed at twelve shillings Scots to the master and the same sum to the doctor, quarterly, for each child. The value of money was so different in those days that it is difficult to realise what that would mean to-day, but it is interesting to see that the Grammar School had two teachers, one of whom is dignified by the title of Doctor.

The Council found it impossible to stop altogether the private schools, so they compromised—how truly British!—to the extent of allowing the Catechism and the Book of Proverbs to be taught in them, but nothing more. It is quite possible that some parents objected to the very long hours in vogue at the public school, which were 6-9, 10-12, and 2-6! The school was regularly inspected by members of the Kirk Session, Town Council and University. The particular needs of the girls were not looked after till 1723, although, doubtless, they attended the public school along with their brothers. At this date, however, a

Slezer's Old Aberdeen, 1683.

school was opened especially for them, in order that they might learn the science and art of sewing and needlework. The Town Council agreed to pay twenty pounds Scots, to enable the mistress to live.

It was represented to the University in 1738 that " the want of an accomplished gentlewoman for teaching white and coloured seam was an occasion of several gentlemen's sons being kept from this College, their parents inclining to send them where they might have suitable education for their daughters also." The University judged it reasonable to advance twelve pounds Scots to a Mrs. Cuthbert " residing in this town who had given sufficient proof of her capacity and diligence."

Some time in the 18th century the original Grammar School disappeared, and was succeeded by the building in School Road, known to many generations of boys as " The Barn." It consisted of one room, to which wings on either side were added later. In that one room about forty boys, from twelve years old and upwards, received their education. Most of the pupils remained for about five years, but many lads of more mature age came for only six months or so, before the Bursary Competition in November. Some of these pupils were bearded men, who had spent their lives on farms, studying in every spare moment and laying by every penny they could spare in the hope of some day " winnin' to the College." Can we wonder that the Barn turned out magnificent results, with such material to work on? The old Grammar School had, at various times, as Rectors men whose names were

household words in the North of Scotland. The most
famous of these are Ewen Maclachlan, who was also
Librarian to the University, Mr. Fyfe and Dr. Dey.

The Gymnasium in the Chanonry was a boarding
school as well as a day school. It attracted boys from
the surrounding district as boarders, and many day
boys came from Old and New Aberdeen. The rivalry
between the two schools, the Gymnasium and the
Grammar, found vent in many pitched battles, especially when snow lay thick on the ground. The Gym.
boys were generally outclassed in the Bursary Competition by their rivals from the Barn, but it was their
proud boast that the class prize lists reversed this
priority. From both schools many lads who have
played their part right nobly went forth into the world.

The Old Town shared in an endowment of Dr. Bell,
Chaplain in the East India Service, by means of which
a school for boys and girls was carried on from 1832
till the educational system of the country was put
under the charge of the School Board. Old Aberdeen
now possesses a very fine Primary School, where excellent work is done by a large staff of teachers. Cookery,
laundrywork and needlework are part of the curriculum
for the girls, while the boys are taught carpentry.

When one considers that the children of the professors and ministers required to be educated, that there
was no means of communication between the two
towns, and that families *were* families in those happy
days—a round dozen being no uncommon thing—one
realises that for the children of the professional class
something had to be done in Old Aberdeen for their

primary education. At one time the need was met by one of the masters of the Gymnasium giving up an hour or two every morning to the younger children, whose big brothers attended the school. Very happy mornings these were for the children; I fear that for the unfortunate master they must have been something of a nightmare. To drive the elements of reading, writing, geography and arithmetic into the heads of about twenty small boys and girls, aged from five to nine years, in one room, and that not a large one, was too much to ask of any unfortunate master. I should think Mr. Thomson must have been very glad when a call to a parish relieved him from his class of Old Town children. A school was then opened by two ladies, daughters of a farmer in Dyce, well-educated, highly refined gentlewomen. Their school did splendid work for nearly half a century. Their interest in the children who passed through their hands was very keen, and to the last day of their lives the Misses Bowman could tell you whose birthday it was, and in what quarter of the globe each scattered member of their flock could be found. It was through no weakness of theirs that the school had to be given up; the work done by the Misses Bowman and the high ideal of honour and duty they set before their pupils cannot be too highly praised. Their school was run on old-fashioned lines; they had little sympathy with Montessori and P.N.E.U. systems. They taught the children, however, that there is no royal road to learning, and that the harder the lesson the more honour there was in mastering it. Tramways and 'buses have made communication so easy that now there is no possibility of a school succeeding in Old Aberdeen ; indeed, we may say that the days of private teachers are a thing of the past.

CHAPTER V.

We must now retrace our steps to the very troublous times which came upon our country in the 17th and 18th centuries. The history of the towns of Old and New Aberdeen is indeed very much the history of Scotland from the time of Queen Mary right on to the beginning of the 19th century, when the dread of a French invasion and the preparations for repelling it kept all the coast towns in a state of armed defence. " Ther wes no citie in Scotland which did suffer more hurt than Aberdeen did, nor oftener " in the Civil Wars which shook the country from end to end after the Reformation. The Covenanting struggles were particularly felt in Aberdeen where so many, including the famous " Aberdeen Doctors," refused to sign the Covenant, insisting upon freedom of conscience for everyone. Nine separate times was Aberdeen taken and retaken; the wonder is, not that it did not grow during those centuries but that it was able to survive at all. In all these struggles Old Aberdeen had to bear its share, and its troubles were greatly increased by there being no governing body at its head to look after the interests of the community. We have seen that the Bishop of the Cathedral was also the head of the town; on him fell the duty of choosing suitable men to look after its interests. After the foundation of King's College and University, of which also the Bishop was the head, he could count upon the support of the regents and doctors, so that we need not be surprised when we find in later and more peaceful days that the Town Council of Old Aberdeen was never without at least one professor or principal, either as provost, baillie or councillor. In these bad times, however, of which we are speaking, the town was left without a Council or any means of summoning one. When the Roman Catholic Bishop was succeeded by an Episcopal Bishop, he inherited the duty of looking after the town in things secular as well as spiritual, but the clash of conflicting opinions between the Crown, the Church and the people left long intervals when the Bishop was unable to do anything for his flock. It is impossible for me to give any account of the Civil Wars which raged in our country during the 17th and 18th centuries. Every student of history must be conversant with them, although it is extremely difficult to follow all the intrigues, plots and factions of these troubled times. The Town Council minutes are very brief and scanty, and the fact that two volumes are missing— that from 1617-1634 and that from 1728-1738—makes it more difficult for us to construct the history of our town.

We know that in 1639 Bishop Bellenden had to flee the city, taking with him as much of his furniture and plate as he could carry away. At this time, too, it was considered safer to close the University; Principal, professors and students all scattered.

In 1644 Old Aberdeen was taxed for the outfitting of twelve foot soldiers and one horseman who were to march with Captain M'Nab into England against the

English. " Ilk soldier was furnished with two sarks, coat and breeks, hose and bonnet, bands and shoon, a sword and musket, powder and ball for so many, and others some a sword and pike, and ilk soldier to have six shillings every day for the space of forty days of loan silver." An armed trooper with his horse cost one hundred and eighty-six pounds thirteen and fourpence. Spalding remarks, " Sore was the poor people of the Old Town plucked and poinded to make up these soldiers' charges, whereas some of them had not to [*sic*] buy a loaf." Neither herd nor hire-man was left untaxed; a troop of horsemen was quartered in the town till the money was all paid. We are told that the Baillies had to advance this money out of their own pockets to get rid of the guard. The danger was, however, so pressing that the Council thought it necessary to provide a drill-master at twenty-four shillings a day " to learn the poor bodies to handle their arms, who had more need to handle the plough." An inventory of the town's arms shows " nine firelock guns, ten halberts, two swords and two banderts with two militia muskets, two picks and other two swords, all burnt with the town's Arms."

The 13th of September, 1644, was a day that brought sorrow and doull to both the towns of Aberdeen. On the 12th Montrose with his army marched down Deeside and encamped at Two-Mile Cross. In the morning he demanded peaceable entrance, in order to read His Majesty's Proclamation. A meeting was summoned by the Provost, when an answer was prepared. Montrose's messengers were, according to

Spalding, " causit to drink hardlie, and be the way the drummer was unhappelie slayne." Montrose, " heighlie offendit," fell upon the town. He defeated its army between the Crabstane and the Justice Mylnes and delivered it to his Irish soldiers, who burned and plundered for four days. These soldiers wore in their caps " ane rip of oates." Spalding says, " Oure towne's people began to weir the lyke in ther bonnetis and to knyt to till the knokis of oure yettis the lyke rip of oates; bot it was littill saifgaird to us." He also tells us that he " saw tua corpis careit to the buriall throw the Old Town with wemen onlie, and not ane man amongst them." The outcome of this terrible defeat had been presaged the night before " the moone ross alls reid as blood tuo houris befoir hir tyme." The end of the trouble was not yet, for a very few days later the Duke of Argyll arrived with his army " quhairof thair wes quarterit on poor Old Abirdeen Argile's own thrie regiments." Spalding goes on to tell us that the first night the officers and gentlemen drank up all the ale and " levit upone wort thairefter." The General Assembly of the Church, meeting in Edinburgh in January, 1648, ordered a fast to be held on the first Sunday of the year, that prayer might be offered to Almighty God for the unhappy state of the country. Spalding says that the second Sunday was also ordered to be held as a fast in Old Aberdeen, whereby " the poor people were vexed to death with their continual fastings and thanksgivings."

In 1669 we have the first mention of the Militia. Old Aberdeen provided four men to the Aberdeen Company, called together in consequence of the war with Holland to protect the port and town. These militia-men must, to a certain extent at least, have been sup-plied by the local lairds. Mrs. Helen Cullen, owner of some land near the Don, being a widow was called upon to supply a fifth man. Very soon afterwards she petitioned that " as she is now clothed with a hus-band " the militiaman is unnecessary. Her petition was granted.

Showing the very unsettled state of affairs that all these civil wars had brought about, we find that in 1688 it was necessary to have an armed guard, watch-ing over the town by night, and to have all men capable of bearing arms instructed in their use. A daily rendez-vous of twenty-four of the Old Town's men was called to meet at the bowling green of King's College at three o'clock of the afternoon in order that they might be drilled. In 1782 Lord Shelborne promulgated a plan for arming the principal towns of Scotland. This plan was agreed to by the Town Council, who called for volunteers. A military association was formed, a con-stitution was framed, and officers were appointed. Major Mitchell, formerly an officer in His Majesty's service, was chosen to be Commandant, Captain Gray to be Captain, Hugh Leslie of Powis to be Lieutenant, and Mr. Volum, Convener of Trades, to be Ensign. Seventy volunteers at once joined, a large proportion, as it was estimated that the whole number of able-bodied men was only one hundred and seventy.

Apparently this military association did not last very long, for in 1798, when the dread of a French invasion was at its height, we find that the Provost and Town Council, "having taken under their serious consideration the present danger of the country from the threatened invasion of the French, our inveterate enemy," resolved to recommend to the inhabitants to prepare themselves for rendering personal services in defence of the King and country in the most efficacious manner. The Council recorded their thanks to Provost Leslie for his suggestion of these resolutions and resolved also that they should be published in the " Aberdeen Journal."

A corps of Old Aberdeen Volunteers was formed. The " London Gazette " contained the following announcement :—" Commissions in the Old Aberdeen Volunteer Association—Alexander Matheson, Captain ; Gilbert Gerard, First Lieutenant; Dr. William Jack, Second." Although Alexander Matheson, one of the Magistrates, was nominally the Captain of the Company, the real Commander was Dr. Gilbert Gerard. He was Professor first of Greek and then of Divinity in King's College, and was one of the ministers of St. Machar's Cathedral. He graduated at King's College in 1777, and came back to the Old Town as Professor in 1790, and in 1791 was enrolled as a Burgess. If one may judge of the man from his portrait, one must feel that only a very strong sense of duty and of the necessity for such service would have made Professor Gilbert Gerard accept a commission in a Volunteer Regiment, yet he commanded the Old Aberdeen Volunteers from 1798 till the Company was disbanded in 1802. His accoutrements may be seen in the Museum of Marischal College; the banner of the Company, worked by his daughters, is preserved in King's College Chapel. An excellent account of the Gerard family, written by the late Mrs. Harrower, will be found in the Aberdeen University Review, Vol. X.

It is a truism that history repeats itself, but it is interesting to recall here that the Rev. Bruce M'Ewen, Ph.D., Second Minister of the Cathedral in 1914, was also a Captain in a Territorial Regiment, that as such he joined up with his men at the outbreak of the Great War, and served all through the years of the War. He found it necessary to resign his ministerial charge when he felt in 1916 that the War was not likely to come to an end very soon. After the Armistice he received a unanimous call from the congregation of the Cathedral to the First Charge, made vacant by the resignation of the Rev. Dr. Calder. The strain of the War, alas, proved too much for his strength, and he passed away in 1923—

" Sed miles sed pro Patria."

No such hardships had to be endured by the Old Aberdeen Volunteer Company, under Captain Gerard. The first appearance of this Corps was in 1798 on the occasion of Nelson's victory at the Battle of the Nile, when they marched in front of the Town House and fired three volleys, which, although it was their first attempt at firing, they performed with exactness ! They returned in the evening, and after having fired three more volleys they were entertained by the Provost and Magistrates of the city.

In 1800 they were inspected by the Duke of Gordon and received their Colours from Major-General Hay. In 1802 they decided to join the Aberdeen Volunteers, of whose history a most interesting account is given by the late Donald Sinclair.

CHAPTER VI.

ONE of the duties which had to be undertaken by the Town Council and its officials in those days, when there were no steam hooters and whistles making morning hideous, was to arouse the sleepers from their beds and get them started to their work. Early hours were evidently the order of the day, if one may judge from the time when the children went to school and the students to their studies, so that some sort of wakening was very necessary. Up to the middle of the 17th century this was accomplished by a bell-ringer, who went through the town at 5 a.m. to rouse the people for their daily work, and again at 9 p.m., when, the day's duties done, it was evidently considered that all good town's folk should be at home and in bed. In 1662, however, the Treasurer was ordered to buy a suit of clothes with a pair of shoes for the Drummer, to whom evidently this duty had been handed. He must have looked very fine indeed, as his suit consisted of " ane long coat of ane purple collour with quhyt lace therupon with breiches and stockings of that same collour, and ane pair double solled shoes." One would have thought he would have been only too glad to show off these beautiful clothes, but perhaps familiarity bred contempt for, in 1687, there were many complaints against him for not doing his duty. The Baillies therefore enacted that if he should anyways fail in doing his duty by not going through the town

and beating the drum " ilk morning and evening at
the ordinar times and seasons, useit and wont, the
weather being dry and he in health " ! that twelve
pennies of his salary shall be retained every day by
the Trades. In 1830 it was decided to use a bugle
instead of a drum, but that cannot have been found so
satisfactory, for one of my earliest recollections is of
watching the drummer marching up the High Street,
attracting the attention of the citizens by his shouts of
" Oyez, Oyez, Oyez," and then announcing that something had been lost or found.

I have referred to the difficulty in which the town
was placed when it had no governing body. In 1690
the Magistrates and Town Council appealed to the
Privy Council, asking that they might be confirmed
in their places and given authority to watch over the
affairs of the town. Their petition was granted, and
the privilege was conferred in 1719 by King George I.,
and again in 1729 by George II., in a Charter, giving,
granting and committing to them the usual and necessary powers within the said Borough . . . With
power to them by a majority of voices yearly to elect
their own successors " aye and while We, our Heirs
and Successors see fit to revoke the forsaid power or
give any other direction in the said matter."

Being thus confirmed in their positions the Provost
and Town Council looked after the interests of Old
Aberdeen for almost two hundred years, when an Act
of Parliament decreed that Old Aberdeen must cease
to exist as a separate community. But more of this
hereafter. Meantime we are concerned with the manner

in which the Provost and Baillies carried out their duties. In 1728 there was a vacancy in one of the Cathedral charges, when the Kirk Session appealed to the Town Council to join with them and the masters of the College in a deputation to the Presbytery, to ask for a free choice in the election of a minister. The Town Council agreed and appointed some of its members to join the deputation. It was right enough that the Town Council should have a voice in the choice of a minister, as they sat in the Cathedral in a loft or gallery of their own. Not only that, but on the occasion of a new Provost taking his seat, it was the custom for them to march up to the Cathedral from the Town House, for the " Kirking of the Council." As the professors also attended divine worship in the Cathedral it was much to their interest also to have a suitable minister.

I have already alluded to the water difficulty, which became fairly acute in the 18th century. The water springs to the west of Old Aberdeen were acquired from the University, but it was felt that a reservoir for the water was absolutely necessary. The Town Council, after visiting the ground floor of the prison, agreed that it was not only the most commodious place for the purpose but that its use would save " a deal of expense to the town." The plan was approved, and it was resolved that the prison be upon the third storey, the second storey being used for meetings of the Town Council and Trades. Apparently the plan was not so economical as our good Fathers had hoped, for by the end of the 18th century they accepted an estimate of three hundred and thirty pounds to rebuild the Town House.

There was evidently great need for economy at this time. The Council decided that, considering the small funds of the town, they were unable to pay the entertainments usually given on certain occasions, especially on the nights of the two markets. It was decided, therefore, to pay four pounds Scots to the men that mounted guard, which could be used by them as they thought proper.

In 1796 the Provost informed the Council that a roll of inhabitants had been taken which showed that there were eleven hundred persons in Old Aberdeen, and that the value of their rents was five hundred and forty pounds fifteen shillings. The Provost went on to point out that many complaints had been received as to the badness of the streets and lanes of the city, and that the only money available was required for the lighting of the streets in winter. He said it was very desirable to have the streets properly causewayed, that they ought to have a foot pavement, and better lighting. He therefore suggested that the inhabitants should assess themselves for twenty-one years at the rate of one shilling per pound of their rents, in order to pave and light the streets and supply the city with water. He also suggested that trustees be appointed by those who contributed to carry out the scheme. This proposal was unanimously agreed to, and a vote of thanks was passed to the Provost, Hugh Leslie of Powis, for the amount of trouble he had taken in this affair.

The proposed union of King's and Marischal Colleges caused our Town Council much anxiety. The first hint of this suggestion reached them in 1786, when they " fully and maturely considered the plan," and came unanimously to the opinion that it would not be productive of the advantages " it set furth," but, " on the contrary, will be hurtful to the country and pre-judicial to the interests of education "; and seeing that this scheme cannot be brought about without the subversion of the chartered rights of a venerable University which has subsisted in our city for near three centuries with honour and reputation, " We, the Provost, Magistrates and Council, must express our disapprobation," etc., etc. They resolved to send a copy of the present " Act " to the Right Hon. Lord Sydney, Secretary of State, and further they decided " to make every legal and constitutional opposition to so unpreceedented and ruinous a measure."

The scheme is not mentioned again in the Town Council minutes for nearly a hundred years. In 1854 the Town Council addressed a Memorial to the Earl of Aberdeen, Prime Minister, pointing out how closely they have watched the measures that have been taken for effecting a union between King's College and Marischal College. In this Memorial they point out that they regard the University and College as the chief ornaments of their city, and the sources of its prosperity ; they look with jealousy on any interference with the privileges which, through a succession of ages, have been transmitted to them. They are quite sensible of the anomalous position which the two Colleges hold

among the Universities of Scotland ; they point out the
advantages of New Aberdeen for the study of Law and
Medicine and the advantages of Old Aberdeen for the
Faculty of Arts. They conclude by expressing their
entire confidence in Lord Aberdeen's knowledge of the
subject and in the integrity and sincerity which have
distinguished his whole life as a Peer of Parliament and
as a Minister of State.

The union of the Universities was carried through
in 1858, very much in the manner suggested by Old
Aberdeen. For many years the appearance of the Old
Town was not changed by the union. Want of
accommodation, however, led to the necessity of new
buildings. New King's was erected on the site of the
Aulton Brewery, which brewed such famous ale. An
old friend living in the High Street lamented its parting
sorely in these words, " We would hae been better
wantin' the University than wantin' the brewery " !
So much for the privilege of living in a University
town.

Further extensions are being carried on meantime,
owing to the very rapid increase in the number of
students since the union, and since the admission of
women to the privileges of University training. A
beautiful new hall for examination and other purposes
is rapidly nearing completion.

The union of the Universities preluded a union
which meant even more to the little community of Old
Aberdeen. For long the Town Council had been faced
with the great difficulty — indeed, one may say the
impossibility—of raising sufficient funds for lighting,

policing, and bringing water to the town. The higher standard of living required that water be brought to the houses, and the suggestion that bathrooms were a necessity was even being hinted. The supply of water was very much limited owing to the purchase by the Great North of Scotland Railway of the ground where the springs were situated. People demanded that the street lamps be lighted every night in winter, whereas the Town Council had funds to do so only when no moon was expected !

The charitable funds in which Old Aberdeen has always been wealthy attracted from the poorer parts of Aberdeen some of the less desirable inhabitants, and it was found that the half policeman, which was all the Town Council could afford, was not sufficient. To add to these difficulties, democracy began to raise its head even in conservative Old Aberdeen, and there was a demand from some of the more advanced young men that they should have a choice in the election of the Town Council, thus striking at the very roots of our ancient constitution. Under the circumstances the Town Council thought it better to call a public meeting and lay the whole matter before the people. The impossibility of imposing higher taxes or of improving the public services as things stood was pointed out, while the advantages of union, better paved roads, better lighting, and a better water supply were demonstrated. It was decided to take a plebiscite of the inhabitants, with the result that 100 voted for amalgamation, 126 against, while 42 did not answer at all. In 1887, however, Old Aberdeen agreed to amalgama-

tion under certain conditions, and in 1891, under an
Act of Parliament incorporating it with Aberdeen, it
ceased to have an independent existence.

In appearance Old Aberdeen has not changed much,
although of late years many houses have been built
in the immediate vicinity. High Street, Chanonry,
and Don Street remain much as they have done for
long. The Cathedral Towers and King's College
Crown are still our distinctive feature, while the much
more modern Powis towers and gateway give a very
quaint touch to College Bounds. Powis towers give
rise to much speculation, and no one can say what was
the idea in the mind of their designer. Some attribute
their curious architecture to the rage for Byron and
all things Eastern at the beginning of the 19th century,
when they were built. The crescent on the top is the
family crest of the Frasers from whom the Leslies of
Powis were descended. The quaint, old Hermitage
upon its hill, so long a feature of Old Aberdeen, is now,
alas! no more, and with it have passed away the many
legends, more or less fanciful, which tried to account
for it.

I cannot conclude this chapter on Old Aberdeen
better than by quoting the following poem by Dr.
Arthur Johnston, 1685 :—

THE OLD TOWN.
(Vulgarly) called Old Aberdeen.

A pious Bishop lives and rules in thee.
Don makes thee prosperous,
And the neighbouring sea.

Don by a wondrous bridge is overlaid,
Of one arch, which the Gods belike have made.
Such was the Rhodian Coloss work of old,
Where ships with hoised sails to pass were bold :
Near this the salmon swim, and snares are set
For them, and they are catcht in every net.
In thee an old and stately temple stands,
The rest demolisht are by strangers' hands :
That temple with two towers doth rise, which be
(as Pharos guids) to travellers at Sea :
Phoebus and Pallas Palaces not far,
From that fair Temple to be viewed are.
Buildings fit for these guests and over them
There is a guilded cross and diadem.
An Holy Bishop raised this Fabrick, which
The King did with fair revenues enrich.
And Rome which doth by words her bounty show
Did names of Honour upon them bestow.
So many Greeks (who ruined Troy by force)
Did not brake forth out of the Trojan horse :
As that brave house of Learning hath brought forth,
Of Shining lights, and men of greatest Worth.
Thou dost not need thy Praises should be sung
Thou Noble Town by any Stranger's tongue;
Since by this people who reside in thee,
Thine Honour fitly published can be.

ST. MACHAR'S CATHEDRAL

It must be quite evident to anyone who has read the foregoing pages on Old Aberdeen that the town owed its very existence to the Cathedral Church of St. Machar. I have already alluded to the legend which caused St. Machar to settle here and build the first little church.

Nectanus, who had been Bishop in Mortlach for some fourteen years, was the first Bishop of the Cathedral, but what sort of a church he came to we have no idea. Boethius tells us that St. Machar built a chapel where the present Cathedral now stands. Neither Nectanus nor his two immediate successors did anything towards building a new church. It was not till 1163 that Bishop Matthew Kininmonth began to build a church which he hoped would be more worthy of its position, and which he intended to dedicate to the memory of St. Machar. This Bishop Matthew Kininmonth had been the Archdeacon of the Cathedral in St. Andrews. To him Malcolm IV. granted a Charter giving to the Cathedral Church " the haill vill of Old Aberdeen with the kirk of Kirkton and the pertinents," also many other kirks in the neighbourhood, also the tithe of the King's " own revenues and all the escheats belonging to me betwixt the two waters called Dee and Spey." This Charter was confirmed by

William the Lion, who added to it " the land of Brass, now called Birse, with the forest thereof."

Matthew Kininmonth's Church was pulled down by Bishop Henry Cheyne on the ground that it was not " glorious enough." He began another church which shared the same fate at the hands of his successor, Bishop Alexander Kininmonth, 1357-1381. This Bishop Alexander Kininmonth was the second of the name. The first Alexander Kininmonth succeeded Bishop Cheyne in 1327. He built two Episcopal palaces, one to the east of the Cathedral and another at Fetternear. The latter was probably for use as a summer residence and also to allow the Bishop to make closer acquaintance with the large district over which he presided. The palace in the Cathedral grounds was burned in 1333, when the English soldiers set fire to Aberdeen, which burned for six days. In 1357 Alexander Kininmonth the Second was created Bishop of the Cathedral. His first step was to pull down part of the edifice and to begin a building on a larger scale than had been contemplated before. To raise funds for this purpose the Dean and Chapter had been collecting for some years, and had themselves contributed sixty pounds a year from their stipends. It is interesting to note that Barbour, author of " The Bruce," was one of the Chapter at the time. The Pope made a liberal grant of indulgences, and King Robert the Bruce himself, who never forgot what he owed to his loyal subjects in Aberdeen, gave as much help as he could. But in spite of all these efforts the money collected was sufficient only to raise the walls of the nave a few feet above the ground, when Alexander Kininmonth died. The work seems to have been at a standstill till 1424, when Henry Leighton, Bishop of Moray, was appointed to the See. He completed the walls of the nave, built St. John's Chapel in the north transept—in which 17 years later he was buried—and built the twin towers. The good work was carried on by his successor, Bishop Lindsay, who paved the church with freestone and roofed it with red fir. Bishop Spens, who was translated from Galloway, was the keeper of the Privy Seal. We are told that he was a man of " an active spirit." His first step was to repair the Bishop's palace, but he was far from unmindful of the church. He erected stalls in the chancel, along with a beautiful chair for the Bishop's use, and he put glass in the windows which must have been an enormous boon to the congregation !

Bishop Spens was succeeded by Bishop Elphinstone, the most famous of all our Bishops. He built the great central tower, of which, alas, we have no picture, and he covered the roof with lead. Orem tells us that the great tower whose foundations had been laid by Bishop Leighton fifty-nine years before " was built four-square and four storey high. It contained a little four-cornered chamber, above which was a square tower with a stang on the top of it, five ells in length, with a great globe of brass above the first cross of the said stang; and above the second cross was a cock, an ell in length, of brass and his breast of copper, which stang, globe and cock Mr. David Corse, a Presbyterian minister of this church, disposed of.''

As Orem wrote about 1725 and the great tower stood
till 1688, there is every reason to believe his account.
In the tower Elphinstone hung three great bells and
many smaller ones, and to his efforts we owe the fact
that the whole roof was covered with lead, which
proved a great temptation later.   Elphinstone now
turned his attention to the condition of the choir, which
Robert the Bruce is reported to have condemned as
unworthy of so great a Cathedral.   The Bishop died,
however, before he had finished his work, broken-
hearted by the misery brought upon Scotland by the
fatal field of Flodden.   His clergy, inspired by his
example, finished the choir and built the high altar.
Bishop Gavin Dunbar, 1519-1532, built the south
transept, which was called his aisle.   He added spires
to Bishop Leighton's twin towers, and he ceiled the
church with " the finest oak, of such excellent work
that there is scarce any like it to be seen in this
Kingdom."   Tradition says that this wonderful roof
cost eight pounds, Scots money, a large sum in those
days.   For a full account of the Cathedral roof I
must refer my readers to the description given by
Principal Sir William Geddes in the volume of the New
Spalding Club called " The Heraldic Ceiling of the
Cathedral."

The   roof   is   adorned   with   forty-eight   shields,
arranged in three rows.   The centre row shows the
shields of His Holiness Pope Leo X., the thirteen
Bishops of Scotland, the Prior of St. Andrews, and the
Arms of the University.   To the right are the shields
of Charles, Emperor of the Holy Roman Empire, thir-

Interior of St. Machar's Cathedral.
(From old print.)